Pebble®
Plus

Cheerleading

Cheerleaders in Action

by Jen Jones

Consulting Editor: Gail Saunders-Smith, PhD

Consultant: Lindsay Evered-Ceilley
Director of Business Operations
Centerstage Starz Theatre and Dance Studio
Centennial, Colorado

Pebble Plus is published by Capstone Press,
151 Good Counsel Drive, P.O. Box 669, Mankato, Minnesota 56002.
www.capstonepub.com

Books published by Capstone Press are manufactured with paper
containing at least 10 percent post-consumer waste.

Library of Congress Cataloging-in-Publication Data
Jones, Jen.
 Cheerleaders in action / by Jen Jones.
  p. cm.—(Pebble plus. Cheerleading)
 Includes bibliographical references and index.
 Summary: "Simple text and photographs describe the origins of cheerleading and what today's cheerleaders
do"—Provided by publisher.
 ISBN 978-1-4296-5274-2 (library binding)
 1. Cheerleading—Juvenile literature. I. Title. II. Series.

LB3635.J616 2011
 791.6'4—dc22   2010028060

Editorial Credits
Jenny Marks, editor; Ashlee Suker, designer; Wanda Winch, media researcher; Laura Manthe, production specialist,
    Sarah Schuette, photo sylist; Marcy Morin, scheduler

Photo Credits
All photos Capstone Press/Karon Dubke except: AP Images/Robert E. Klein, 17; Minnesota Historical
    Society/Minneapolis Journal, 9; Shutterstock/Ekaterina Shavaygert, glitter background, Molodec, star
    background; University of Minnesota Archives, 7, 11

Note to Parents and Teachers

The Cheerleading set supports national physical education standards related to movement
forms. This book describes and illustrates what cheerleaders do. The images support early
readers in understanding the text. The repetition of words and phrases helps early readers
learn new words. This book also introduces early readers to subject-specific vocabulary words,
which are defined in the Glossary section. Early readers may need assistance to read some
words and to use the Table of Contents, Glossary, Read More, Internet Sites, and Index
sections of the book.

Printed in the United States of America in North Mankato, Minnesota.
092010
005933CGS11

Table of Contents

Faces of Cheer

Today there are more than
4 million cheerleaders
in the United States.
Cheerleading has changed
a lot over the years.

History of Cheer

Cheerleading began more than 130 years ago. The first cheerleaders were students at Princeton University and the University of Minnesota.

University of Minnesota
cheerleaders, 1919

A few guys decided to lead

the crowd in some cheers.

They used short sayings like,

"Rah, Rah, Rah! Ski-um-bah!"

In 1923 girls began joining cheer squads. They added motions and dance steps to cheers. Some used pom poms and signs.

Cheerleading Today

Over the years, cheer became a sport. Today's cheerleaders don't just yell. These athletes dance, tumble, and do stunts while cheering.

Kids as young as age 6 can be cheerleaders. They join a cheer squad at a cheer gym. Older students can cheer for school sports teams.

Cheer gyms put together all-star cheering squads. All-stars perform only at cheer competitions. The best squads win trophies.

Many of today's cheerleaders
are on all-girl squads.
Other teams have both girls
and boys. A squad with both
is called "co-ed."

Spirit All Around

There are many kinds
of cheerleaders. But one
thing is true of them all.
They have amazing spirit!

Glossary

all-star—a kind of cheerleader that does not cheer for sports teams; all-star cheer squads compete against each other to win cheer contests

athlete—one who participates in a sport

co-ed—including both boys and girls

competition—a sporting event where two teams meet to see who is the best

motions—movements done while cheering

perform—to sing, dance, do stunts, or cheer in front of others

squad—a team of cheerleaders

stunt—a daring physical activity

tumble—to do gymnastics moves

Read More

Gassman, Julie. *Cheerleading Really Is a Sport.* Sports Illustrated Kids: Victory School Superstars. Mankato, Minn.: Stone Arch Books, 2011.

Jones, Jen. *Cheer Gear.* Cheerleading. Mankato, Minn.: Capstone Press, 2011.

Karapetkova, Holly. *Cheerleading.* Sports for Sprouts. Vero Beach, Fla.: Rourke Pub., 2010.

Internet Sites

FactHound offers a safe, fun way to find Internet sites related to this book. All of the sites on FactHound have been researched by our staff.

Here's all you do:

Visit *www.facthound.com*

Type in this code: 9781429652742

Check out projects, games and lots more at
www.capstonekids.com

Super-cool stuff!

23

Index

Word Count: 184
Grade: 1
Early-Intervention Level: 15